z^ZZ

Wake up, pup!
Do you really
want to sleep
the day away?

2

But puppies like to play! Get out there and have fun!

BEST FRIENDS *FUR-EVER*

Puppies frolic with other puppies for many of the same reasons you play with other kids. Playtime teaches young pooches important lessons in how to make friends—and keep them.

That's more like it! Look at you!

Those puppy-dog eyes!

That soft, fluffy body!

That wrinkly face!

No doubt about it,

puppies are ...

7

SO CUTE!

It's TRUE.

Puppies are rarely born alone. Instead, they enter the world in groups called litters.

SPECIAL DELIVERY

If you think one puppy is cute, imagine 24 of them, all snuggling with each other against their mother! That's the number of puppies born to a Neapolitan mastiff in 2004—a world record! The mastiff is a big breed of dog. Typically, larger breeds have bigger litters of pups than smaller dogs.

Puppies are helpless fluffballs when they're born. They can't even open their eyes for their first week!

Is somebody talking? HELLO?

13

Puppies are born without teeth.
They grow a set of baby teeth
that they lose just like you do.

My bark is worse than my BITE.

You can't even BARK yet!

15

Puppies need lots of sleep. They snooze **15** to **20** hours a day! All that shut-eye helps them grow up fast.

DOG DAYS

The first six months in a typical pup's life:

ONE DAY OLD: Puppies are born blind, deaf, and without any teeth.

ONE WEEK OLD: After a week of doing little more than sleeping and eating, puppies double in size.

TWO WEEKS OLD: They open their eyes and can hear.

THREE WEEKS OLD: Puppies can finally stand up and stumble around. Some even start wagging their little tails.

FOUR WEEKS OLD: Their teeth come in, and they start chewing on everything.

SIX MONTHS OLD: This big boy has his permanent set of teeth, is sleeping a lot less, and is playing a lot more!

But when they wake up,
puppies are ready to play!
Puppies play by chewing,
chasing, and rolling around.

Sometimes puppies have too much fun— and get into trouble.

TIME-OUT, PUP!

Just because puppies are cute doesn't mean they don't misbehave—although it's not entirely their fault. Chewing helps them ease the ouch of new teeth coming in. Unfortunately, puppies don't know the difference between a chew toy and your shoes. They eventually learn what they're allowed to chew on as they grow older.

But
I'm still a
GOOD BOY,
right?

21

Puppies don't always look like the grown-up versions of their breeds. For example, Dalmatian puppies are born without spots.

PUPPY PARADE!

There are more than 400 breeds of dogs (and puppies!). Here are some of the more common ones.

Bichon frise

Chihuahua

Bichons frises and Chihuahuas never outgrow your lap.

Hey, Mom, have you seen my SPOTS?

Australian shepherd

Labrador retriever

Great Dane

Bernese mountain dog

Australian shepherds and Labradors grow into brainy dogs that love to work.

Great Danes and Bernese mountain dogs grow from teeny to gigantic in about two years.

Puppies love you as much as you love them. They bond with the person who cares for them the most!

PUPPY PALS

Puppies and people go way back—as far back as 30,000 years ago, when humans began tossing bits of food to wolves in return for protection and help with hunting. All that quality time together paid off. Studies show that dogs can understand our tone of voice and facial expressions. People become happier and more productive when they spend time with dogs.

You and me, we're A TEAM.

25

Studies show that puppies love being talked to. They especially love baby talk.

Studies also show that puppies reach peak cuteness at around two months old, which is when they're usually adopted as pets.

You humans do a lot of WEIRD STUDIES.

Puppies technically become dogs when they reach their first birthday, but that doesn't mean they'll stop being your best friend!

I'm a
BIG DOG
now!

31

NATIONAL GEOGRAPHIC and Yellow Border Design are trademarks of the National Geographic Society, used under license.

Since 1888, the National Geographic Society has funded more than 14,000 research, conservation, education, and storytelling projects around the world. National Geographic Partners distributes a portion of the funds it receives from your purchase to National Geographic Society to support programs including the conservation of animals and their habitats. To learn more, visit natgeo.com/info.

For more information, visit nationalgeographic.com, call 1-877-873-6846, or write to the following address:

National Geographic Partners, LLC
1145 17th Street N.W.
Washington, DC 20036-4688 U.S.A.

For librarians and teachers: nationalgeographic.com/books/librarians-and-educators

More for kids from National Geographic: natgeokids.com

National Geographic Kids magazine inspires children to explore their world with fun yet educational articles on animals, science, nature, and more. Using fresh storytelling and amazing photography, *Nat Geo Kids* shows kids ages 6 to 14 the fascinating truth about the world—and why they should care.
natgeo.com/subscribe

For rights or permissions inquiries, please contact National Geographic Books Subsidiary Rights: bookrights@natgeo.com

Written by Crispin Boyer
Designed by Julide Dengel

Hardcover ISBN: 978-1-4263-3906-6
Reinforced library binding ISBN: 978-1-4263-3907-3

The publisher would like to thank everyone who worked to make this book come together: Rebecca Baines and Ariane Szu-Tu, editors; Shannon Hibberd, photo editor; Molly Reid, production editor; and Anne LeongSon and Gus Tello, design production assistants.

PHOTO CREDITS:
AL = Alamy Stock Photo; AS = Adobe Stock; GI = Getty Images; SS = Shutterstock
Cover: (UP LE), gillmar/SS; (UP RT), Mark Taylor/Nature Picture Library; (LO LE), Adogslifephoto/Dreamstime; (LO CTR), 101cats/GI; (LO RT), Dorottya Mathe/SS; spine, Andrey_Kuzmin/SS; back cover: (LE), Ermolaev Alexandr/AS; (RT), svetography/AS; 1, Eric Isselée/AS; 3, otsphoto/AS; 5, Orientgold/SS; 6, Paul Park/GI; 6-7, Grigorita Ko/AS; 7, annette shaff/AS; 9, Dmytro Synelnychenko/AS; 10, Geoff Robinson/SS; 11, Lisa Van Dyke/GI; 13, Andy Crawford/Dorling Kindersley/AL; 14, Veronica Morley/EyeEm/GI; 15, Spaces Images/GI; 16, Kevin Monaghan/EyeEm/GI; 17 (UP LE), Andy Crawford/Dorling Kindersley/AL; 17 (UP RT), Maya Karkalicheva/GI; 17 (CTR LE), Colin Seddon/Minden Pictures; 17 (CTR RT), H. Mark Weidman Photography/AL; 17 (LO LE), Christina Rollo/AL; 17 (LO RT), pomchai7/AS; 18 (LE), otsphoto/AS; 18 (RT), michaelheim/SS; 19, otsphoto/AS; 20, David ODell/SS; 21, LaineN/SS; 22 (LE), mikeledray/SS; 22 (RT), Gorlov Alexander/SS; 23 (UP), SolStock/GI; 23 (LO LE), Alessandra Sarti/AL; 23 (LO CTR LE), Pascale Gueret/AS; 23 (LO CTR RT), O. Giel/Juniors Bildarchiv GmbH/AL; 23 (LO RT), Eve Photography/SS; 24, Chris Stein/GI; 25, Larry Williams/GI; 26 (LE), kali9/GI; 26 (RT), aldomurillo/GI; 27, kali9/iStockphoto; 29, R. Richter/Tierfotoagentur/AL; 30-31, Purple Collar Pet Photography/GI; 32, Ermolaev Alexandr/AS

Printed in China
21/PPS/1

Where do dogs park their cars? IN A BARKING LOT!